Famous Artists

Get to Know John Singer Sargent

Charlotte Taylor

Enslow Publishing
101 W. 23rd Street
Suite 240
New York, NY 10011
USA
enslow.com

Published in 2016 by Enslow Publishing, LLC
101 W. 23rd Street, Suite 240, New York, NY 10011

Library of Congress Cataloging-in-Publication Data

Taylor, Charlotte, 1978- author.
Get to know John Singer Sargent / Charlotte Taylor.
pages cm. — (Famous artists)
Includes bibliographical references and index.
Summary: "Describes the life and work of painter John Singer Sargent"— Provided by publisher.
ISBN 978-0-7660-7230-5 (library binding)
ISBN 978-0-7660-7227-5 (pbk)
ISBN 978-0-7660-7228-2 (6pk)
1. Sargent, John Singer, 1856-1925—Juvenile literature. 2. Painters—United States—Biography—Juvenile literature. I. Title.
ND237.S3T39 2016
759.13—dc23
[B]

2015029911

Printed in the United States of America

To Our Readers: We have done our best to make sure all website addresses in this book were active and appropriate when we went to press. However, the author and the publisher have no control over and assume no liability for the material available on those websites or any websites they may link to. Any comments or suggestions can be sent by e-mail to customerservice@enslow.com.

Portions of this book can be found in *John Singer Sargent The Life of an Artist* by Eshel Kreiter and Marc Zabludoff

Photo Credits: Cover, pp. 1, 4, 27 Heritage Images/Fine Art Images/Getty Images; throughout book Rudchenko Liliia/Shutterstock.com (painting background), Mostovyi Sergii Igorevich/Shutterstock.com (palette and brushes dingbat), foxie/Shutterstock.com (brushstrokes), rzstudio/Shutterstock.com (paint brush); p. 7 HultonArchive/Getty Images; p. 8 John Singer Sargent/Wikimedia Commons/Miss Frances Sherborne Ridley Watts.jpg/public domain; p. 11 Portrait of Carolus-Duran, 1879 (oil on canvas), Sargent, John Singer (1856-1925) / Sterling and Francine Clark Art Institute, Williamstown, Massachusetts, USA / Bridgeman Images; p. 13 © Artepics / Alamy Stock Photo; p. 16 The Print Collector/Hulton Fine Art Collection/Getty Images; p. 19 Spanish Soldiers, c.1902-03 (w/c on paper), Sargent, John Singer (1856-1925) / Brooklyn Museum of Art, New York, USA / Purchased by special subscription / Bridgeman Images; p. 21 Bedouin Camp, 1905-06 (w/c on paper), Sargent, John Singer (1856-1925) / Brooklyn Museum of Art, New York, USA / Bridgeman Images; p. 22 Portrait of Madame Gautreau, 1883-1884, (oil on canvas) , Sargent, John Singer (1856-1925) / Metropolitan Museum of Art, New York, USA / De Agostini Picture Library / Bridgeman Images; p. 25 © Bygone Collection / Alamy Stock Photo; p. 28 Universal History Archive/Universal Images Group/Getty Images; p. 30 Tate, London/Art Resource, NY; p. 33 ACME imagery/Superstock; p. 35 Theodore Roosevelt (colour litho), Sargent, John Singer (1856-1925) (after) / Private Collection / Peter Newark American Pictures / Bridgeman Images; p. 36 © AP Images; p. 39 Gassed, an oil study, 1918-19 (oil on canvas), Sargent, John Singer (1856-1925) / Private Collection / Photo © Christie's Images / Bridgeman Images; p. 41 David L. Ryan/The Boston Globe/Getty Images.

Contents

Chapter 1

Growing Up in Europe

John Singer Sargent was famous for painting portraits of rich and powerful people. Although these portraits made him rich, he loved painting landscapes and murals as well. Sargent is known as a great American artist, but he spent most of his life in Europe.

Sargent was born on January 12, 1856, in Florence, Italy. His parents, FitzWilliam and Mary, had gone to Europe after their first child, a daughter, died. John's father thought they would stay away from America for just a little while, until Mary felt better. But they never moved back.

John and his younger sisters, Emily and Violet, spent their entire childhood in Europe. They moved often. In the winter, the family went someplace warm, such as Italy or southern France. In the summer, they found a cooler spot, like the mountains of Switzerland or Germany.

The children quickly grew used to different countries and different languages. By the time John was a teenager, he could speak French, German, and Italian nearly as well as English.

John felt comfortable in all the countries of Europe. But he never really felt at home in any of them. Mostly that was because he never stayed in one place long enough to make any close friends.

Early Learning

Usually, John played by himself or with Emily. He liked running around outdoors a lot more than sitting inside and studying. School might have been a big problem for him—if he had gone. Luckily for him, his parents and tutors taught him at home. His father was his teacher for reading, science, and math. His mother taught him music and art.

Mothers usually know quite a lot about their children, and John's mother was no exception. But even she could not know that John would one day become a great artist. By chance, though, she taught him to be one.

Mary Sargent told her son to always carry a sketchbook with him. She asked him to draw whatever he saw, from city scenes to country landscapes. He drew the crashing waves of the ocean and the flowing waves of tall grass in the field.

Growing Up in Europe

John Singer Sargent was born to American parents in Florence, Italy, shown here. He and his family traveled around Europe a lot when he was a child.

Portrait of Frances Sherborne Ridley Watts (1877, Philadelphia Museum of Art). Sargent met "Fanny" Watts when he was a boy growing up in Europe. He painted this picture of his friend when he was in his twenties.

He drew almost every place he ever lived in or visited, every hillside, every beach, every town square.

John learned to amuse himself by drawing instead of playing with friends, and he got into the habit of drawing for many hours every day. It was a habit he had for his entire life. He also learned to entertain himself with music. This was in the days before there were any CDs, tapes, or even radio. To hear music, someone had to play an instrument. John wanted to hear music often, and so he became an excellent pianist.

Chapter 2

Art School

As John got older, he realized that he wanted to paint all the time. His parents had never planned for him to be an artist. They saw art and music as something all children should learn, like reading and writing. But when John was eighteen, he decided that it was time he learned how to be a real artist. He went to study in Paris, the center of the art world.

In Paris, John Singer Sargent went to a school that was run by the artist Carolus-Duran. Sargent's teacher recognized his talent right away, and so did the other students. Sargent's paintings were the best in the school, and he quickly became one of his teacher's favorites.

Art schools are like other schools. Students often resent the teacher's favorite. So it would not have been surprising if Sargent's classmates had disliked him. Most of the other students actually liked him, though. They admired his hard work.

Portrait of Carolus-Duran (1879, Clark Art Institute, Williamstown, MA). Carolus-Duran was Sargent's teacher in Paris.

Art Smarts

Sargent's 1879 painting of his teacher, Carolus-Duran, helped make him a well-known portrait artist. Art critics praised Sargent's use of color—the yellow coat, gray background, and hint of blue of the chair. Those who knew Carolus-Duran also stated that Sargent captured the teacher's expression perfectly.

Painting People

As Sargent studied with Carolus-Duran, he began to focus on portraits—paintings of people. This turned out to be something Sargent was especially good at doing. He was able to capture someone's personality in a single painting. The people in his paintings look like they have just stopped for a moment to tell us a quick story.

When he was twenty years old and still an art student, Sargent finally saw the United States. His mother thought it was a good time for a visit. It was 1876, and that Fourth of

Dr. Pozzi at Home (1881–1882, Armand Hammer Museum of Art and Cultural Center, Los Angeles, CA). As a young artist, Sargent tried hard to make his paintings stand out. In this portrait, the outfit worn by his subjcct is meant to catch the eye.

July was the country's one-hundredth birthday. He met his uncles, aunts, and cousins for the first time. This was the first of many visits to America for Sargent. Sometimes he would stay for more than a year, but he never stayed for good. He always went back to Europe.

Chapter 3

The Portrait Artist

Paris was the most important city in the world for art. And the most important art event in Paris was the Salon. All of the artists wanted their work displayed at this show, which was held every year in May. The Salon was enormous—room after room jam-packed with art, with sculptures crowding the floors and paintings climbing the walls right up to the ceiling. Thousands of people came to see the artworks exhibited, and the artists all hoped they would be noticed and launched into stardom.

Sargent had paintings in the Salon by the time he was twenty-one, and they were noticed right away. All the critics predicted a great future for him. When Sargent was twenty-three, he exhibited his portrait of his teacher. The painting was so good that Carolus-Duran realized there was nothing more he could teach Sargent. It was time for Sargent to go out on his own.

Carnation, Lily, Lily, Rose (1885-86, Tate Britain, London). In this oil painting, Sargent's subjects were his friend's daughters, aged seven and eleven.

Sargent had certainly grown up. He was about six feet tall, broad-shouldered, and serious-looking. He had a full beard and moustache. He made a point of dressing like a grown-up, too. Unlike some of the other students, he wore a jacket, vest, and tie all the time, even when he painted.

Sargent's Subjects

Sargent painted portraits for two reasons: He was good at it, and he enjoyed it. But he also wanted to make money. And in the 1880s, many people were happy to pay to have their portraits painted. A portrait made them seem important. It showed other people that they were rich and powerful. Naturally, they were eager to have the best artists paint them. Just as naturally, they usually were not eager for the artists to be completely true to reality. They often told the artists just how they wanted to look when the painting was done.

The men thought they should look solid, serious, and dependable. They thought their wives should look beautiful and their children smart and well-behaved. Mostly, they wanted to look like all the other rich people they knew. They did not want to look unusual in any way.

Sargent wanted to make these people happy. He needed them, and their wealthy friends, to hire him to paint their portraits. So he tried to make them appear as they wished.

But he could not help being attracted to whatever was out of the ordinary.

Exotic Art

In 1879 Sargent went on a long trip to Spain to search for exotic people and places to paint. From Spain he traveled to North Africa. He went to Morocco and Tunisia. He traveled for days on horseback to reach a small village just because he had heard it was full of interesting buildings. He drew and painted everything he saw.

Art Smarts

Even though most of his portraits were done in oils, Sargent also painted more than two thousand watercolors in his life. Sargent liked to use watercolors because of the way they helped him capture the effects of light. His use of watercolors helped to give many of his paintings a dream-like feel.

Spanish Soldiers (1903, Brooklyn Museum, New York). Sargent painted this watercolor while he was visiting Spain.

In these paintings he tried to do more than just paint what things looked like. He wanted people to know what it felt like to walk on a hot, dusty Moroccan dirt street or to sit in a dim café in Spain, watching a beautiful young woman dance. He wanted people to imagine the rhythm of the guitars and to hear the sound of the dancer's feet on the wooden floor.

Back in Paris, people liked Sargent's paintings of Spain. (The French did not mind if people in Spain looked unusual.) But Sargent's fondness for exotic people got him into trouble when he met a woman named Virginie Gautreau.

Madame Gautreau

Madame Gautreau was twenty-three and, like Sargent, was an American. But she had lived in France since she was four years old. In her own way, she was a celebrity. She did not actually do anything—she did not sing or dance, for example, or write or paint. But everyone knew her. You could not help noticing Madame Gautreau. She went out of her way to look strange and mysterious. She made her pale skin even paler with lots of white powder. Then she added rose-colored makeup to her ears.

As soon as Sargent saw Virginie Gautreau, he wanted to paint her. He was sure a painting of her would make him famous. And he was right. The portrait he painted of her was his most famous painting. But it was also his biggest headache.

Bedouins (1905, The Brooklyn Museum, New York). Sargent liked to paint pictures of unusual subjects. Bedouins are people who move around from place and place and sleep in tents. This painting was done when he visited Syria and Palestine.

Madame X (1883–1884, Metropolitan Museum of Art, New York). Sargent's painting of Virginie Gautreau caused him a great deal of trouble. He decided to remove her name from the portrait when he sold it, instead simply calling it *Madame X*.

Sargent thought the painting would take him three weeks. Instead, it took months. From the start, Madame Gautreau caused him many problems. First, she would not hold still. Then, he could not find a good pose for her. He drew her sitting, kneeling, reading, playing piano. Nothing seemed right to him.

In the end, he painted her standing, with her head twisted to the side to show off her ear and nose. She wore a black dress, which made her skin look even whiter. The dress was sleeveless, but full length. It left her pale arms, neck, and shoulders bare.

When he was finished, the painting was certainly hard to ignore. Unfortunately, to many people, it was ugly.

People were wildly upset when they saw the painting at the Paris Salon of 1884. Virginie Gautreau hated it. So did her mother, who stormed over to Sargent's studio and yelled at him. She thought the portrait made her daughter look disgraceful. She was sure that it made people want to laugh at them. Many of those who saw it agreed.

Part of the problem was her dress. The French have a word for this kind of dress: risqué, which means a bit risky. People thought the dress showed too much bare skin. When Sargent first painted it, it was even riskier: He painted one strap slipping off Madame Gautreau's shoulder, so it seemed that the dress would fall down. To calm her mother, Sargent repainted the strap on her shoulder.

The French newspapers made quite a fuss over the portrait. For a long time it was all anyone talked about when they saw Sargent. Finally, he could not stand it anymore, and he left Paris to stay in London for a while. In 1886, when he was thirty, he moved there for good. He thought the English might like his paintings more than the French did. He was right. He soon was busy painting portraits of the rich and famous of England. London became his home for the rest of his life.

In 1885, Sargent posed in his apartment in Paris. His painting *Madam X* had nearly caused a riot at the 1884 Salon.

Chapter 4

Sargent at Work

Sitting for one of Sargent's portraits was not always easy. He had strong ideas about what would make a good painting. He often made his subjects try many different poses. He had them change their clothes again and again. A person might have to pose every day for weeks and weeks before Sargent was satisfied.

Children enjoyed watching him. Although Sargent never married and had no children of his own, he knew how to keep them interested. Sometimes he would dance for them or play the banjo.

It was a good thing he could keep the children happy. They had to be just as patient as the adults while sitting. One child had to pose eighty-three times before the painting of her was finished.

Sargent traveled a great deal, but London was his home from 1886 until his death. This is a 1907 photo of the famous Tower Bridge.

Sargent's paintings were an enormous success. By the 1890s he was the most famous portrait painter in England and the United States.

In 1898, he did twenty portraits. A portrait could easily require about forty sittings. The jobs began taking up all of his time.

The Rich and Famous

Most of Sargent's portraits were of women. All were rich and many were either famous themselves or were married to famous men.

Art Smarts

Many artists begin a picture by doing something called underpainting. This is a first layer of the painting, when the artist lays out the main shapes and colors before painting over them with oils. Sargent often skipped this step. That way, he had more freedom in painting his subjects as he saw them in the moment. He could make them look more natural.

Henry G. Marquand (between 1900 and 1912, Metropolitan Museum of Art, New York). Sargent made a living painting portraits of wealthy people. The subject of this portrait, Marquand, was a rich American art collector.

Ena and Betty, Daughters of Asher and Mrs. Wertheimer (1901, Tate Gallery, London). Sargent became close to the Wertheimer family as he painted twelve portraits of them over a period of ten years.

Part of the portrait artist's job was to make his models look even more beautiful and more confident than perhaps they really were. Another part of it was to surround them with objects of value and class. But Sargent had the unusual ability to show a person's personality in the portrait as well.

Some of the famous men Sargent painted were the American writers Henry James and Robert Louis Stevenson, French artist Claude Monet, and Frederick Law Olmstead (who designed New York's Central Park). He did portraits for many members of England's aristocracy—that is, people with titles such as duke, baron, earl, or lord.

Most of the people Sargent painted were very rich. They lived in a world of huge houses and servants. But they did not all belong to the same world. Some, like the Wertheimer family, were "outsiders."

The Wertheimers were a large, wealthy family, but they were not really accepted as part of English high society. That was because they were Jewish. At the time, not everyone in England thought Jews should be treated as equals.

Sargent, however, liked the Wertheimers. He did not pay much attention to their being Jewish. He saw them as people who were interesting to paint and fun to be with. Perhaps Sargent felt at ease with the Wertheimers because he always saw himself as an outsider also. His portraits of them are among the best he ever did. They are bright and lively. He especially liked one of the daughters, Ena (short for Helena). She became a friend of his for the rest of his life.

Difficult Subjects

Not all of Sargent's subjects were as pleasant as the Wertheimers. Some fussed and fidgeted. Some whined and whimpered and pouted as well as any six-year-old. They complained about how long Sargent took to finish the painting. They found little things they did not like. They asked Sargent to change the way their mouth looked, or their eyes. Sargent sometimes needed a lot of patience to not get too annoyed, and after many years of painting portraits, he found it harder and harder.

Sargent did more than five hundred portraits in all. He influenced an entire generation of portrait artists. He documented the rich and famous people of his day. It is interesting to look back and see how people saw themselves at that time.

Mr. and Mrs. Isaac Newton Phelps Stokes (1897, Metropolitan Museum of Art, New York). Sargent began this portrait intending to paint the wife and her Great Dane. But when the dog was not available to sit for the portrait, the woman's husband offered to take its place.

Chapter 5

Beyond Portraits

Sargent was very successful as a portrait artist. But he began to grow tired of painting people. In 1907, at the age of fifty-one, Sargent decided he had had enough. No more portraits, he promised himself. He did not need the money. By painting hundreds of portraits of the rich, he had become rich himself. He had also become so famous that King Edward VII of England wanted to make him a knight. He politely said no. To accept the honor, he would have to give up being a citizen of the United States, and Sargent would not do that. He might live in England, but he always thought of himself as an American. Sargent now wanted to spend the rest of his life working on paintings he thought were more important than portraits.

He could not keep his promise completely. There were some people to whom he just could not say no. He felt he

Theodore Roosevelt (1903–1904, The White House, Washington, DC). Sargent did not want to paint President Roosevelt, but he could not refuse the honor. He did not enjoy being ordered around by people while he was painting. This became Roosevelt's official White House portrait.

Frieze of Prophets, North wall (installed 1895, Boston Public Library Murals). Sargent painted a series of murals at the Boston Public Library from 1890 to 1919. It is not considered his best work, although Sargent was very proud of it.

had to paint United States presidents Theodore Roosevelt (in 1903) and Woodrow Wilson (in 1916) when he was asked. (Who could say no to the president of the United States?) And he painted a portrait of industrialist John D. Rockefeller. (Who could say no to one of the richest men in the world?) But even Rockefeller had to almost beg Sargent to do it before he said yes.

A New Project

Mostly, though, Sargent spent the rest of his life working on other kinds of paintings. He spent many years on an enormous project for the new public library in Boston, painting a huge picture on the library ceiling. He had begun working on it in 1890. He worked on it on and off for thirty years, traveling back and forth between the United States and England.

The library painting was different from all the other work Sargent had done. In the portraits and in the paintings and drawings he did while traveling, Sargent painted real people and real places. But for the library painting he thought he could do more. He called his painting *The Triumph of Religion.* He thought he could show thousands of years of history in one painting. This time, he was not painting people as they really lived. He was trying to use pictures to tell a long, complicated story.

Today, most people agree that the library work was not Sargent's best. John Singer Sargent was a great painter. But he did not always realize what he was best at doing.

Last Works

In 1916 Sargent was hired by the Museum of Fine Arts in Boston to paint murals inside their building and create sculptures. He worked on the museum project during the remaining years of his life. Fortunately, Sargent always did many things at the same time. During World War I, the British government asked him to do a painting of British and American soldiers fighting side by side. Sargent agreed. The only problem was that he had no idea what war really looked like. So he went to France, where the battle was raging, to find out.

What he saw changed his idea of what he should paint. He saw a long line of soldiers, standing outside, waiting to see a doctor. They were all bandaged and hurt. The Germans had used a poison gas that burned the soldiers' eyes and skin. Sargent called his painting *Gassed.* It is twenty feet long and shows more than sixty soldiers.

Gassed was one of Sargent's last great paintings. John Singer Sargent died seven years later, on April 15, 1925, at the age of sixty-nine.

Gassed (1918, Imperial War Museum, London). Sargent created this twenty-foot-long painting after seeing soldiers who had been hurt in World War I.

When he died, newspapers in both England and the United States ran front-page stories about him. The British papers called him a great British painter. Newspapers in the United States called him a great American painter.

Both were right. He always called himself an American. But he spent far less time in America than in England. In truth, though, he did not really live in either place. He lived to paint, wherever he was.

The Daughters of Edward Darley Boit (1882, Museum of Fine Arts, Boston). A young girl gets an up-close look at one of Sargent's famous works. More than a century later, art lovers of all ages still appreciate how Sargent was able to capture the personalities of the people he painted.

Timeline

1856—John Singer Sargent is born in Florence, Italy.

1874—Goes to Paris to study with Carolus-Duran.

1876—Visits United States for first time.

1877—Has first show at the Paris Salon.

1879—Exhibits portrait of teacher and starts life as a professional painter. Travels to Spain.

1884—Exhibits portrait of Virginie Gautreau (*Madame X*).

1885—Visits England.

1886—Makes London his permanent home.

1890—Begins Boston Public Library paintings.

1907—Announces that he will paint "no more portraits."

1914—Start of World War I.

1918—Visits battlefield in France. Paints *Gassed.*

1922—Cofounds the Grand Central Art Galleries in New York City.

1924—The galleries hold a major retrospective exhibit of Sargent's work.

1925—Sargent dies in London at the age of sixty-nine.

1986—The Whitney Museum of American Art in New York holds a retrospective exhibition of Sargent's work.

1999—A traveling show featuring Sargent is held at museums from Boston to London.

2015—The Metropolitan Museum of Art in New York holds an exhibition highlighting Sargent's portraits of friends and artists.

Glossary

critics—People who study or collect or write about art and who judge which art is "good" and which art is not.

document—To record details.

exotic—Very unusual and exciting, often from another country.

high society—People who are important, wealthy, or related to royalty and generally have a lot of influence over the fashions, tastes, and opinions in their country.

landscape—A picture that shows the countryside or other natural scene.

model—A person who poses for a painting or a picture.

mural—A large painting done directly on a wall.

portrait—A painting of a particular person, usually focused on the face.

pose—The position a person must stay in while an artist tries to make a picture or sculpture of him or her.

retrospective—An exhibition that shows the work that an artist has done in the past.

Salon, the—The huge art exhibition that was held every year in Paris during the nineteenth century.

subject—The person or object being painted by the artist.

tutor—A private teacher, often one who comes to a student's home.

Learn More

Books

Brooks, Susie. *Get Into Art: People*. Boston: Kingfisher, 2013.

Frisch-Schmoll, Joy. *Portraits*. Mankato, MN: Creative Paperbacks, 2013.

Gallati, Barbara. *John Singer Sargent: Painting Friends*. New York: Skira Rizzoli, 2015.

Temple, Kathryn. *Art for Kids: Drawing*. New York: Sterling, 2014.

Websites

The John Singer Sargent Virtual Gallery

www.jssgallery.org

Includes the largest online collection of Sargent's works.

The Metropolitan Museum of Art: John Singer Sargent

www.metmuseum.org/toah/hd/sarg/hd_sarg.htm

Provides a biography as well as a slideshow of Sargent's art.

Museum of Fine Arts, Boston: John Singer Sargent Watercolors

www.mfa.org/exhibitions/john-singer-sargent-watercolors

Features a recent exhibition of Sargent's watercolors, including video and slideshow.

Index